The Joy of First Classics

Selected and edited by Denes Agay.

T0039749

Foreword

The Joy of First Classics presents a colorful repertory of easy pieces by master composers, both well-known and lesser-known. Indeed, the student and player will find here numerous names and works not encountered before; music which has been unduly neglected, but deserving – because of its intrinsic musical value – to be included in the teaching repertory of the early-grade student.

The word 'classics' in our title indicates not only the style of the Viennese masters, Haydn, Mozart, Beethoven, and their contemporaries, but, in a broader sense, music which has shown itself worthy of general esteem for a considerable span of time. Certainly, works which have been known, played, and loved for a century (Liszt), or even considerably longer (Bach) qualify to be termed 'classic'.

The pieces are in their original forms. Expression marks, fingerings, were added and, in a very few cases, minor editorial adjustments made to clarify the note-picture and facilitate understanding. Keyboard miniatures of three centuries – musically rewarding and technically the most accessible – comprise the content of this volume; instructive and diverting fare for all beginning and early-grade pianists.

Denes Agay

Exclusive Distributors:
Hal Leonard
7777 West Bluemound Road,
Milwaukee, WI 53213
Email: info@halleonard.com

Hal Leonard Europe Limited
42 Wigmore Street, Marylebone,
London WIU 2RY
Email: info@halleonardeurope.com

Hal Leonard Australia Pty. Ltd.
4 Lentara Court, Cheltenham,
Victoria 9132, Australia
Email: info@halleonard.com.au

This book Copyright © 1987 Yorktown Music Press, Inc.

All rights reserved.
For all works contained herein: Unauthorized copying, arranging, adapting, recording, Internet posting, public performance, or other distribution of the music in this publication is an infringement of copyright. Infringers are liable under the law.

Order No. YK 21376
US International Standard Book Number: 0.8256.8066.2
UK International Standard Book Number: 0.7119.1101.0

Yorktown Music Press, Inc.

Old German Dance ..... Praetorius 4
Canario (Old Dance) ..... von der Hofe 5
Little Sonata ..... Wilton 6
Brave Knight ..... Vogel 8
Aria ..... Speer 8
Follow Me! ..... Chován 9
Four Little Pieces ..... Türk 10
  Entrée 10
  Minuetto 10
  Complaint 11
  Carefree 11
Gavotte ..... Handel 12
Russian Dance ..... Goedicke 13
Two Little Inventions ..... Ryba 14
Gavotte ..... Witthauer 15
Danse Galante ..... Witthauer 15
Two Hungarian Play Tunes ..... Bartalus 16
Bear Dance ..... Schumann 18
The Lute Player (Bourré) ..... Saint-Luc 19
Song Without Words ..... Spindler 20
Exuberance (German Dance) ..... Hüllmandel 21
Carefree Stroll ..... Köhler 22
German Dance ..... Haydn 23
Dance Song ..... Sporontes 24
Duettino ..... Hässler 25
Old English Air (Felton's Gavotte) ..... Felton 26
Mazurka ..... Szymanowska 27
Minuet ..... J.S. Bach 28
Russian Folk Song ..... Beethoven 29
Tarantella ..... Clark 30
La Montagnarde (The Highland Girl) ..... Mouret 31
Minute K.6 ..... W.A. Mozart 32
Bagatelle ..... Diabelli 33
Musette ..... J.S. Bach 34
Minuet ..... L. Mozart 35
Pastorale ..... Burgmüller 36
Bourrée ..... Krieger 37
Village Dance ..... Beethoven 38
The Cuckoo Waltz ..... Müller 39
Mount Vernon Set ..... Reinagle 40
  Intrada 40
  Promenade 40
  Minuet 41
  Quadrille 42

Cradle Song ..... Kirnberger 43
Christmas Pastorale (The Shepherds' Call from Bethlehem) ..... Rathgeber 44
Ecossaise ..... Beethoven 45
Arabesque ..... Burgmüller 46
Waltz ..... Schubert 47
Sonata (Minuet) ..... Scarlatti 48
Early English Sonatina ..... Duncombe 49
Air ..... Purcell 50
Bourrée ..... Graupner 51
Russian Polka ..... Glinka 52
Circle Dance ..... Le Couppey 53
Contredanse ..... Unknown 54
Rondino Pastorale ..... Reinecke 55
Alexander March ..... Beethoven 56
Scherzino ..... Reinecke 57
Rondino ..... Rameau 58
Elegy ..... Reinecke 59
Carnival ..... Couperin 60
Rigaudon ..... Telemann 61
Allegro *K.3* ..... W.A. Mozart 62
Solemn Procession ..... Pieyel 63
Rondoletto ..... Brunner 64
Carillons ..... Kirnberger 65
King William's March ..... Clarke 66
Canzone ..... Türk 67
Ländler ..... Schubert 68
Little Piece (from Album for The Young) ..... Schumann 69
L'Epineuse (The Thorny One) ..... Couperin 70
Arioso ..... Telemann 71
Burlesca ..... Telemann 71
Sonatina No. 2 (1st Movement) ..... Latour 72
Gigue ..... Tischer 74
Dance Sonatina ..... Attwood 75
Romantic Story ..... Gurlitt 76
Playful Dialogue ..... Hummel 77
Waltz ..... Schubert 78
Ecossaise ..... Kuhlau 79
Album Leaf ..... Liszt 80

Old German Dance

Michael Praetorius
(1571 - 1621)

Canario

Old Dance

Joachim von der Hofe
(about 1612)

Little Sonata

1. Moderato

C. H. Wilton
(18th Century)

2. Minuetto

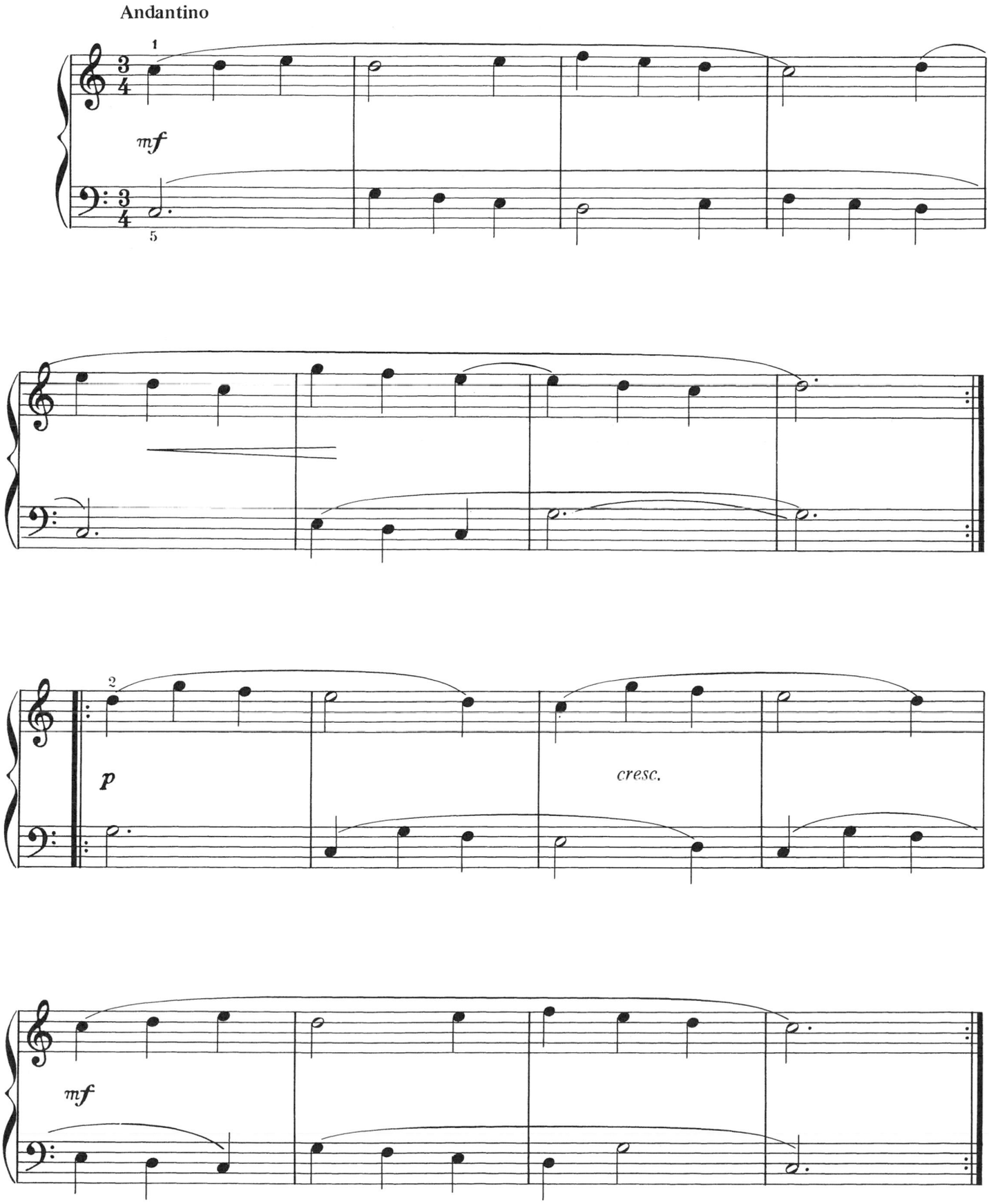

Brave Knight

Moritz Vogel
(1846 - 1922)

Aria

Daniel Speer
(1636 - 1707)

Follow Me!

Kálmán Chován*
(1852 - 1928)

Allegretto

* Pronounced KHO-vahn. Hungarian composer and influential pedagogue.

Four Little Pieces

1. Entreé

2. Minuetto

3. Complaint

4. Carefree

Gavotte

George Frideric Handel
(1685 - 1759)

Russian Dance

Alexander Goedicke
(1877 - 1957)

Two Little Inventions

1.

Jan Jakub Ryba*
(1765 - 1815)

Moderato

mp

mf

D.C.

2.

Andante

p

mf

p

D.C.

* Pronounced REE - bah. Czech composer of many works, mostly vocal.

Gavotte

Johann Georg Witthauer
(1750 - 1802)

Andante

p

cresc.

mf

p

mf

Danse Galante

Johann Georg Witthauer
(1750 - 1802)

Andantino

mf

Two Hungarian Play Tunes

1.

István Bartalus
(1821 - 1899)

2.

Bear Dance

from the sketch book for Album For The Young

Robert Schumann
(1810 - 1856)

The Lute Player

Bourré

Jacques Saint - Luc*
(1616 - 1689)

* Pronounced San - Lueck. Belgian composer and virtuoso on the lute.

Song Without Words

Fritz Spindler
(1817 - 1905)

Exuberance

German Dance

Nikolaus Joseph Hüllmandel
(1751 - 1823)

Carefree Stroll

Louis Köhler
(1820 - 1886)

German Dance

Joseph Haydn
(1732 - 1809)

Dance Song

* German composer and poet. Famous lyricist and publisher of a collection of popular dance melodies.

Duettino

Johann Wilhelm Hässler
(1747 - 1822)

Andantino

Old English Air

Felton's Gavotte

Mazurka

Maria Szymanowska*
(1790-1831)

Moderato

mf

Fine

p

sf

sf

D.C. al Fine

* Pronounced SHEE-ma-novska. Polish piano virtuoso and composer.
A pupil of John Field, admired by Robert Schumann.

Minuet

From the Little Notebook for
Anna Magdalena Bach *
(1725)

* Johann Sebastian Bach's second wife.

Russian Folk Song

Ludwig van Beethoven
(1770 - 1827)

Vivace

mf *p*

f

p *f*

Tarantella

Scotson Clark
(1840 - 1883)

La Montagnarde

The Highland Girl

Jean Joseph Mouret
(1682 - 1738)

Minuet K.6

Wolfgang Amadeus Mozart
(1756 - 1791)

Bagatelle

Antonio Diabelli
(1781 - 1858)

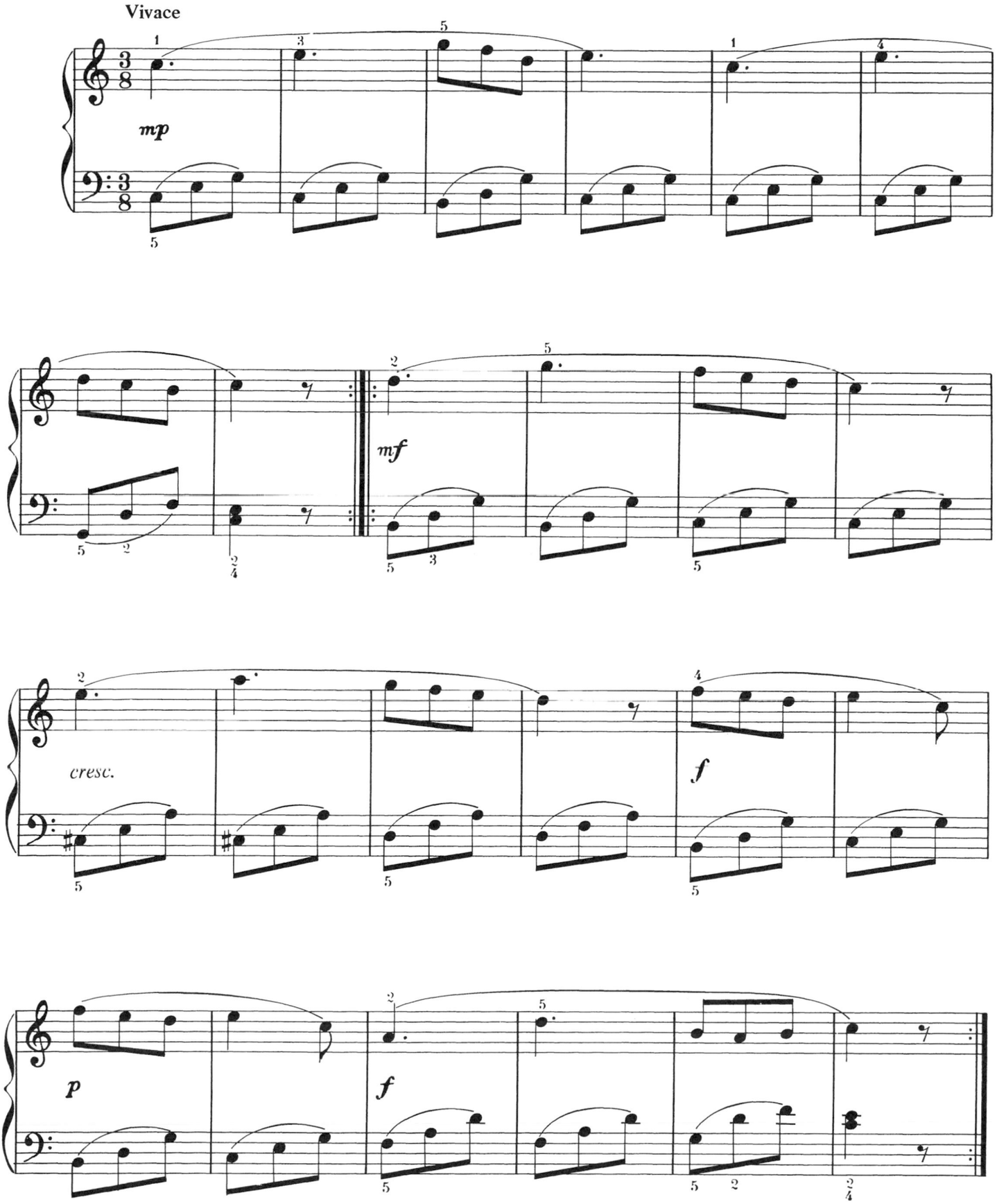

Musette

From the Little Notebook for
Anna Magdelena Bach
(1725)

Minuet

From Leopold Mozart's *
Little Notebook for Nannerl

Andante grazioso

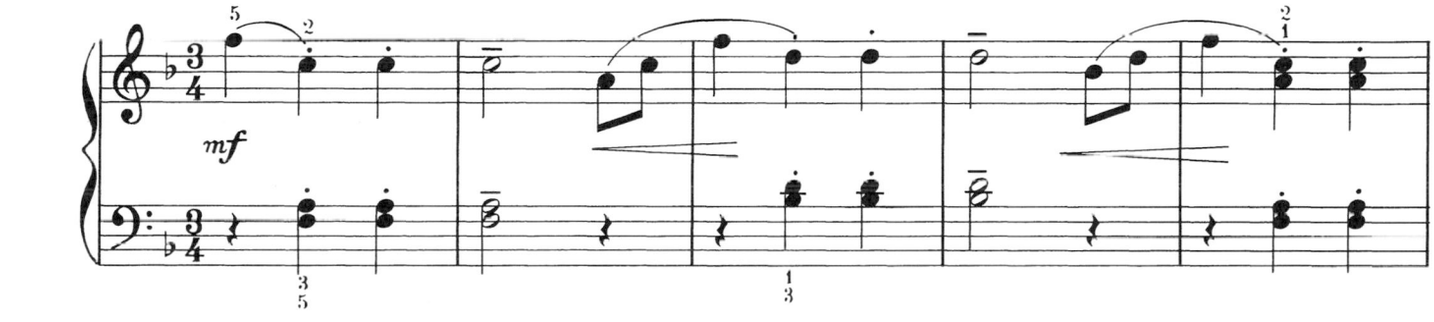

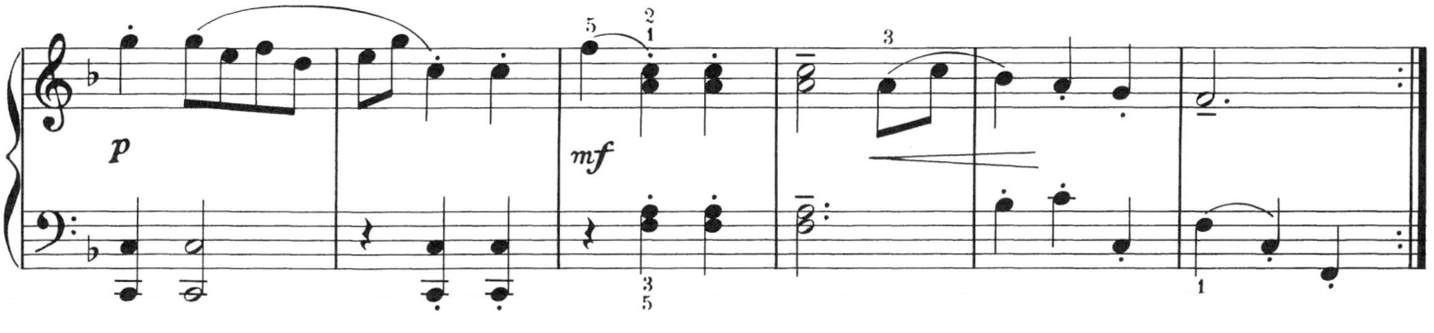

* *Compiled for his daughter Anna Maria, sister of Wolfgang Amadeus.*

Pastorale

Friedrich Burgmüller
(1806 - 1874)

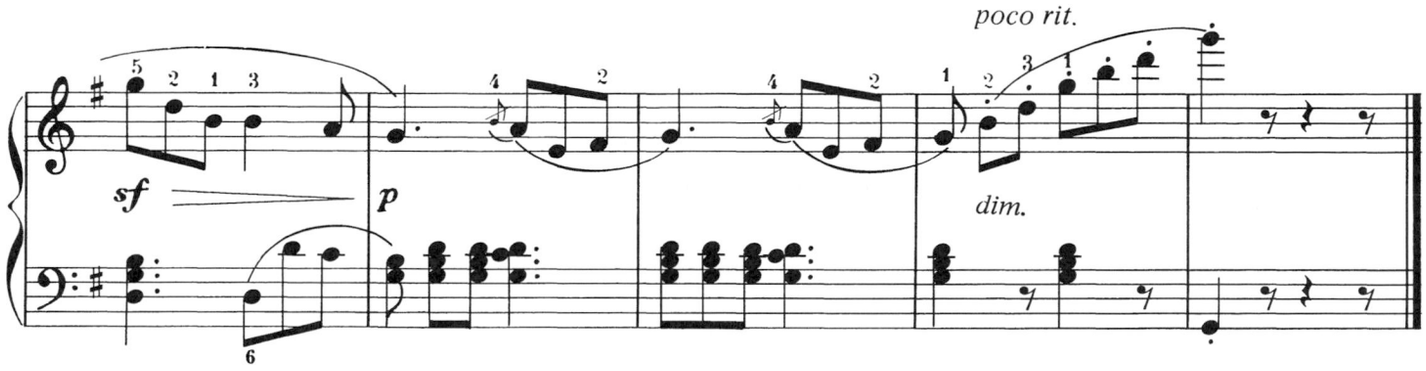

Bourrée

Johann Krieger
(1651 - 1735)

Allegretto

mf (repeat p)

mf

f

Village Dance*

Ludwig van Beethoven
(1770 - 1827)

* From one of Beethoven's sketch - books.

The Cuckoo Waltz

August Eberhard Müller
(1767 - 1817)

Mount Vernon Set

1. Intrada

Alexander Reinagle*
(1756 - 1809)

Allegretto

f

mp *cresc.*

f

2. Promenade

Andantino

mf

f

p *cresc.*

* English composer and teacher who came to America in 1786. Nellie Custis, George Washington's adopted daughter was one of his pupils.

3. Minuet

4. Quadrille

Cradle Song

Johann Philipp Kirnberger
(1721 - 1783)

Christmas Pastorale

The Shepherd's Call from Bethlehem

Valentin Rathgeber
(1682 - 1750)

Ecossaise

Ludwig van Beethoven
(1770 - 1827)

Allegro

f sf sf sf sf

(mf) f mp

1. 2.

mp

1. 2.

Arabesque

Friedrich Burgmüller
Allegro scherzando
p
cresc.
mf
1.
2.
mf
poco rit.
dim.
a tempo
p
cresc.
p
1.
2.

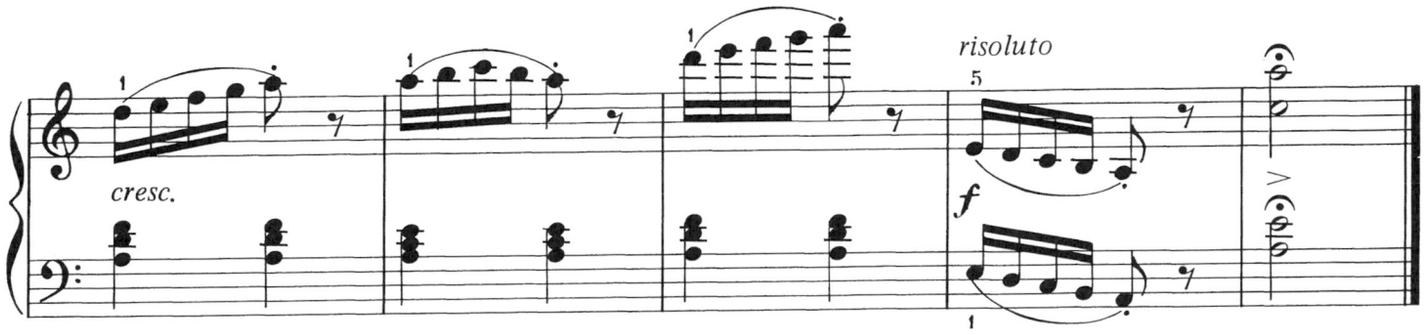

Waltz

Franz Schubert

Moderato

p

1. 2.

mf

Sonata

Minuet

Andantino

Domenico Scarlatti
(1685 - 1757)

Early English Sonatina

William Duncombe
(18th Century)

Air

Henry Purcell
(1658 - 1695)

Bourrée

Christophe Graupner
(1683 - 1760)

Russian Polka

Mikhael Ivanovich Glinka
(1804 - 1857)

Circle Dance

Felix Le Couppey
(1811 - 1887)

Contredanse

Unknown French Composer
(18th Century)

Rondino Pastorale

Carl Reinecke
(1824 - 1910)

Alexander March

Piano version by
Carl Czerny

Ludwig van Beethoven
(1770 - 1827)

Scherzino

Carl Reinecke
(1824 - 1910)

Allegretto marziale

Rondino

Moderato

Jean Philippe Rameau
(1683 - 1764)

Elegy

Carl Reinecke
(1824 - 1910)

Andante con moto

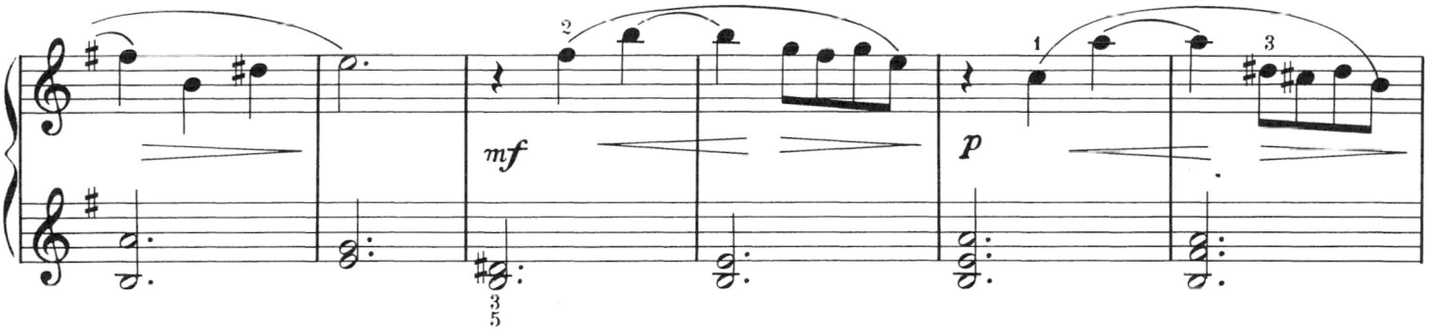

Carnival

François Couperin
(1668 - 1733)

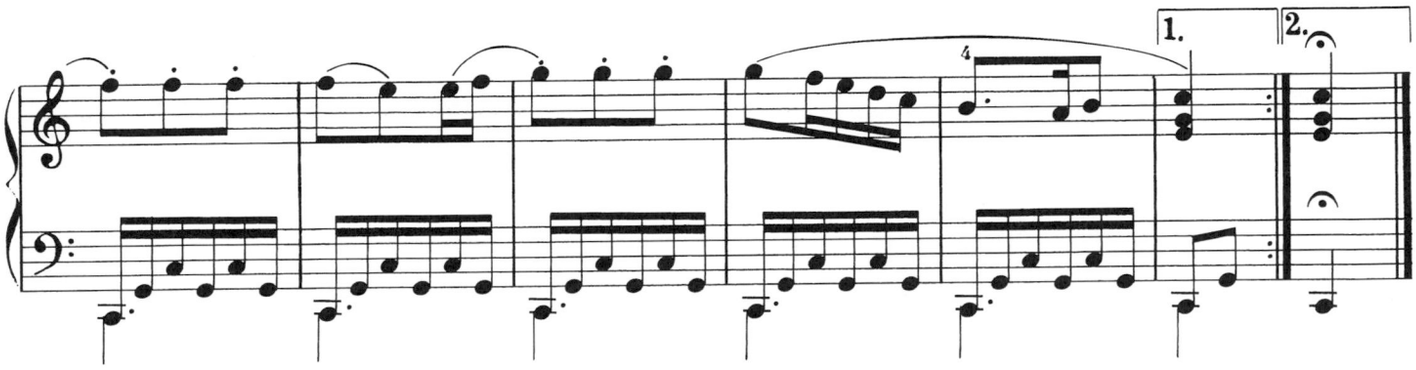

Rigaudon

Allegretto

Georg Philip Telemann

Allegro K.3

Wolfgang Amadeus Mozart
(1756 - 1791)

Solemn Procession

Ignaz Pleyel
(1757 - 1831)

Rondoletto

Christian Traugott Brunner
(1792 - 1874)

Carillons

Johann Philipp Kirnberger
(1721 - 1783)

King William's March

Canzone

Daniel Gottlob Türk
(1756 - 1813)

Andantino

Ländler

Franz Schubert
(1797 - 1828)

Little Piece

from Album For The Young

Robert Schumann
(1810 - 1856)

Moderato

L'épineuse*

The Thorny One

François Couperin
(1668 - 1733)

* *Theme and First Couplet*

Arioso

Georg Philipp Telemann
(1681 - 1767)

Grave

mf

Repeat *p*

Segue Burlesca

Burlesca

Allegretto

Georg Philipp Telemann

mf

mp

cresc.

f

mf

Sonatina No. 2

1st Movement

Jean (T.) Latour
(1766 - 1837)

rit.
a tempo
mf
dim.
p
mf
p
mf
f

Gigue

Johann Nikolaus Tischer
(1731 - 1767)

Dance Sonatina

Thomas Attwood
(1763 - 1838)

Romantic Story

Cornelius Gurlitt
(1820 - 1901)

Playful Dialogue

Johann Nepomuk Hummel
(1778 - 1837)

Waltz

Franz Schubert
(1797 - 1828)

Ecossaise

Friedrich Kuhlau
(1786 - 1832)

Album Leaf

Printed in the E.U.